AF882325

Copyright © 2022 Carolyn Goodwin

All rights reserved. No part of this book may be reproduced in any form on by an electronic or mechanical means, including information storage and retrieval systems, without permission in writing from the publisher, except by a reviewer who may quote brief passages in a review.
First Edition

Carolyn Goodwin
https://1stgenerationfinance.com
www.carolyngoodwincpa.com

ISBN 978-1-7377276-0-6 (paperback)
ISBN 978-1-7377276-1-3 (e-book)

Front cover image photography by Hayley Goodwin

Carolyn Goodwin, CPA PLLC ©

Dedication

To my children, Hayley, and Conner:
You all are my inspiration for creating this book. I pray that this will be a baseline for you both in understanding how to manage what God has and will give you.

To my husband, Brad:
Thank you for your encouragement through the process of creating this book and for continuing to teach our children about money and how the financial world works.

To my mom, Joyce, and my late father Clifford:
Thank you for setting an example of how to manage finances and instructing me to be responsible with a credit card early in life.

Carolyn Goodwin, CPA PLLC ©

About Carolyn

Carolyn is a busy wife, mother, business owner, and homeschool mom. She has a passion for helping youth gain an understanding in financial literacy.

She started homeschooling her children and incorporating money and finance into their studies and daily life. Over time she has turned her love for teaching and desire to provide financial literacy to other children into creating her first *Personal Finance Basics: Curriculum for Beginners, Middle School, and High School* curriculum.

Carolyn earned her undergraduate degree with a Bachelor of Science in Accounting at Longwood University in Farmville, Virginia. Carolyn became licensed as a CPA in 2001 and is currently licensed in North Carolina and South Carolina. She has over 20 years of experience in the accounting profession. Carolyn owns her own practice, Carolyn Goodwin, CPA PLLC and has an online learning platform, 1st Generation Finance.

Carolyn Goodwin, CPA PLLC ©

Table of Contents

Student Finance Commitment

I will do my best in completing the assignments and lessons in this finance course.

I will carefully and responsibly budget and consider where my money will go after earning it.

I will plan for my future and set goals necessary to help me use my God-given talents and abilities.

____ Student Signature

Carolyn Goodwin, CPA PLLC ©

Carolyn Goodwin, CPA PLLC ©

1ST GENERATION
FINANCE
A DIVISION OF CAROLYN GOODWIN, CPA PLLC

Parent/Guardian Finance Commitment

I will assist and engage in the finance assignments set forth in this finance course.

I will guide my child in a plan to give, save, and spend his/her money as he/she receives it.

I will assist my child in exploring his/her God-given talents and gifts to be used currently and in the future.

____ Parent/Guardian Signature

Carolyn Goodwin, CPA PLLC ©

Lesson 1

Talents & Gifts

"'For I know the plans I have for you,' declares the Lord, 'plans to prosper you and not to harm you, plans to give you hope and a future'." Jeremiah 29:11 (NIV)

Since the beginning of time, God has had a plan for each of our lives. He knew what he had planned for us before we were formed in our mother's womb. That is amazing! God has given each of us special gifts and talents to be used to bring Him glory. The key is to use what He has given us. As we explore your gifts and talents in this section, I encourage you to pray with your parents or guardians over what it is God has for you to do. As I am here with you right now, I am praying that prayer for you as well.

There are a few terms to become familiar with when deciding which path, you would like to take...college, job, or career. For those obtaining an education beyond high school you have several educational degree levels to decide on. You will find some vocabulary words that are good to know below.

Vocabulary Words to Know

- A **career** is an occupation someone has for a long period of a person's life with opportunities to move up or progress
- A **job** is a specific duty, task, or activity someone completes using his or her time, skills, and energy
- **Entrepreneurship** is defined as the activity of setting up a business or businesses in which one takes on financial risks in the hope of profit

There are several factors that play a role as to which career or job one may choose. One of the main factors that come to mind is how much income can be earned in a particular field or job. A person may be very qualified for a position but may choose another path based on factors that are not income related. Some of those factors could be job satisfaction, for example. How fulfilling is that job going to be? Independence is another reason. This is a common reason the entrepreneurial path is chosen by some people. They would like to have control over their time and ability to make as much or as little money as they would like. There are some careers or jobs that will give more freedom and flexibility than others. Others choose based on their family situation or location. Someone with children may choose a totally different job than someone without children due to greater family responsibilities. There are also jobs and careers that are more prevalent in certain locations, and one may not believe moving to another area would be a good fit for them. Risk is another factor. There is risk in choosing a career or job. Will going to college and getting a degree for this career or job be worth it financially?

Education is Important – 4 Main Degree Levels

> "Getting wisdom is the wisest thing you can do! And whatever else you do, develop good judgment". Proverbs 4:7 (NLT)

Invest in yourself. This is a term that is familiar to some. If not, this refers to attaining education and training as it relates to your job or career. Education and training are especially important, and the costs and benefits (for example, income that can be earned over time) should be highly considered. There are immediate costs when pursuing any education and training. If those costs outweigh the future benefits reconsideration should be considered as this would not be cost beneficial. However, when the future benefits outweigh the costs, it would be appropriate to pursue the education or training that is being sought after.

This applies to education degrees. When graduating from high school, there is the option to obtain further education or to wait. It is important to obtain education whether planning to go to college or not. It could be in a field you would like to study or a trade you are interested in pursuing. In the highly competitive job market, we believe education and training is a benefit regardless. If you are thinking about not obtaining additional education or training, write out an assessment of your decision. List the pros and cons but do not forget about listing out the future benefits of obtaining higher education and/or training. Wages and salaries can vary among workers in the same position based on individual education and training. The more training or education you have, the more income you may be able to earn.

There are several degrees of education. We start off in elementary school then go to middle school and from there we go to high school. After high school, there are many degrees that can be earned. They are:

- Associates Degree - These are 2-year programs that may provide the student with training for entry-level (beginner) positions. These degrees are mostly available at community and technical schools. These degrees can transfer to a 4-year university to continue the education of the student.

- Bachelor's Degree – This program generally takes 4 years to complete. A major area of study needs to be chosen in this program. This program provides the student with qualifications to work in entry or management positions. The Bachelor's Degree is generally available at college and university schools; however, technological advances today have made bachelor's degrees available on-line at various schools.

- Master's Degree – A bachelor's degree is usually needed to enter this program. It usually takes 1-2 years to complete. Students will become specialized in an area of study in this program. The Master's Degree is generally available at college and university schools; however, technological advances today have made master's degrees available on-line at various schools.

Carolyn Goodwin, CPA PLLC ©

- Doctoral Degree (PhD) – This is the most advanced type of degree and generally require the student to have a master's degree. This program usually takes several years to complete. The graduates are qualified to work as experts in business or as researchers and professors.

Carolyn Goodwin, CPA PLLC ©

YOUR CALL TO ACTION

- Read Matthew 25: 14-30 and talk to your parents about a career assessment of your choice. A few sites are listed below to get you started.

    - https://www.123test.com/career-test/index.php - Free
    - https://www.16personalities.com/
    - https://www.48days.com/disc/ - This test is not free, but it is incredibly detailed and helpful. Choose the classic profile.

- Go to the Occupational Outlook Handbook on the web at https://www.bls.gov/ooh/. Look up the career and/or job that you have an interest in and read more about it. Gather valuable information in a chart to help you write or illustrate your career plan below. Note the level of education needed for the career/job you research. If you have more than one that you would like to explore, please do so. If you have more than one in a chart, then I encourage you to list out your information and comparisons for easy and quick access. Some examples of what you will need in your chart are:

    - Median Pay
    - Entry level education
    - Work experience
    - On-the-job training
    - Job Outlook
    - Employment change

*Please note: You will continue this project throughout the duration of this course so keep this handy.

Carolyn Goodwin, CPA PLLC ©

- Research colleges and technical schools of interest. Review and write out or print the admissions requirements and costs to attend. Compare the immediate cost and future benefits for your job or career of choice. Use manilla folders or a file folder on your computer and make one for each college of interest. Keep this folder to collect information about each college. Save this folder for your time in high school. Add and take away folders as needed. As the folders are narrowed down, these will be schools you will want to schedule college tours when you are a Junior in high school.

- Interview three individuals in different jobs or careers and ask them if there were any non-income factors that influenced their job or career choice. Write a 3-paragraph paper based on your interviews. Include any non-income concerns for a career or job of choice that you may have as well.

Carolyn Goodwin, CPA PLLC ©

LESSON EXTENSION

Volunteering, Internships, and Job Shadowing

Even though you may not be of age to get a job or start a career there are several ways in which you can gain valuable knowledge and experience in the career you desire to pursue. Below are three ways you can accomplish this.

1) Volunteering – A volunteer is someone who donates his or her time and skills without expecting monetary payment in return. The time volunteered affords you the opportunity to learn a new skill or strengthen a skill you already have.

2) Internship – An internship is an opportunity to apply the knowledge you have gained from your school in a workplace setting. An internship can either be paid or volunteer.

3) Job Shadowing – This is an opportunity to observe a person do his or her job. You will get to see exactly what it is like to work in the career field of your interest.

YOUR CALL TO ACTION

- As you explore the career field of your interest, think of ways you can gain additional experience and exposure with either of the opportunities above.
- Seek out someone in the career field you would like more information about with your parents/guardians. Ask if there are any opportunities available to volunteer, intern, or shadow.

Carolyn Goodwin, CPA PLLC ©

Lesson 2

Income, Taxes, & Deductions

"Give to everyone what you owe them: If you owe taxes, pay taxes: if revenue, then revenue; if respect, then respect; if honor, then honor." Romans 13: 7 (NIV)

Now that we have explored the difference between careers and jobs, we are ready to look at what to do with your money after you have earned it through working or investments (**earned income**). Some types of income include a **salary** (a fixed payment that is normally paid monthly or bi-weekly mostly expressed as an annual amount of money); **business income** (income from owning your own business), **rental income** (income that is collected from the use of another person's property); **investment income** (income that comes from interest payments, dividends, capital gains, which will be discussed in chapter 6; **capital appreciation** (a difference between the purchase price and selling price of an investment; **wage** (a regular fixed payment paid daily or weekly); **tip** (money earned in addition the base price of a service given to a customer); **commissions** (money paid when a task is completed; usually when selling a certain amount of goods or services); **social security** (discussed later in this chapter); and **governmental assistance** (money received from the government as a form of income).

Salary is a common form of income that we will be exploring. We will be looking at what to expect when receiving a salary from an employer. We will explore the paycheck and how to read one. If you look at a paycheck you may ask, "What exactly does a paycheck look like and what are all of those numbers that are deducted (or taken out) of my pay?" The most asked question when getting one's first check is "what happened to the money I calculated I would receive in my check?"

In addition to income earned, employers may offer fringe benefits. Fringe benefits are often included in your compensation plan. They are benefits that compensate employees related to their work or for job satisfaction. Some of those fringe benefits include life, disability, and health insurance, educational assistance, and or tuition reimbursement if an employee is in school. Others may be retirement plan contributions, health savings account, gym memberships or discounts.

You have more than likely experienced sales tax through your day-to-day purchases of items from the store and other places. Sales tax is used for state and local purposes. Police, fire protection, libraries, zoos, jails, museums, and other designated uses are ways sales tax is used to name a few.

In our economic system, taxes are also taken out of the money we earn as well. Yes, you read correctly. You do not get to take home the **gross pay**, (the amount you earn before taxes and other deductions) you take home your **net pay** (the amount of your check after taxes and other deductions). The state you live in, and the federal government get some of the money you earn each pay period. **Payroll deductions** are money that is taken out in addition to the federal and state income taxes you must pay on the money you earned. They may include money for retirement into your company 401k, health insurance payments your employer takes out of your check, or a savings account to put aside money only for medical reasons as discussed later. A paycheck will look something like this:

Carolyn Goodwin, CPA PLLC ©

Company Name
Company Address

EARNING STATEMENT

EMPLOYEE NAME / ADDRESS	SSN	REPORTING PERIOD	PAY DATE	# 9698
Employee Name Employee Address	XXX-XX-1234	02/22/2017 - 02/28/2017	03/01/2017	Employee # 7859

INCOME	RATE	HOURS	CURRENT PAY	DEDUCTIONS	TOTAL	YTD TOTAL
GROSS EARNING	$20	40	$800.00	STATUTORY DEDUCTIONS		
				FICA-MEDICARE	$11.60	$104.40
				FICA SOCIAL SECURITY	$49.60	$446.40
				FEDERAL TAX	$108.10	$972.90
				STATE TAX	$40.00	$360.00

sample

YTD GROSS	YTD DEDUCTIONS	YTD NET PAY	TOTAL	DEDUCTIONS	NET PAY
$7,200.00	**$1,883.70**	**$5,316.30**	**$800.00**	**$209.30**	**$590.70**

Vocabulary Words to Know

- A **retirement plan** is money that is saved and invested for the future so when one retires this money will be there to spend and live off of.
- A **retirement plan contribution** is an amount of money an employer will contribute towards an employee's retirement plan.

Carolyn Goodwin, CPA PLLC ©

- **Insurance** is a way in which an insurance company guarantees a lump-sum amount of cash for a loss, damage, illness, or death if a premium (an amount of money an insurance company charges for an insurance policy) is paid.

- **Life insurance** provides a lump-sum amount of money that is paid out to a designated person upon the death of an employee or after a set period.

- **Disability insurance** provides money monthly to an employee who is not able to work and earn money due to a disability.

- **Health insurance** provides money to cover medical expenses, dental expenses, and prescription drugs to name a few.

- **Health savings account** is an account an employer gives employees access to save money for expenses related to health care. This money is set aside before taxes are taken out of your check. These are called pre-tax dollars.

- **Cafeteria plan** allows employees to choose from pre-tax benefits. Such as life, disability, and health insurance; health savings accounts; and retirement plans.

- **Flexible spending account** is like a savings account, but it is used for healthcare expenses such as childcare and dependent care expenses. These funds are pre-tax (meaning the money is set aside before federal, state, and FICA taxes are deducted), which will be discussed below. This money must be used on healthcare or dependent care expenses by the end of the year. Some employers may extend the end of year requirement to a few days into the new year.

In the example above, note the gross pay reported on the earnings statement is $800 but the net pay is $590.70 (the amount the employee takes home). You will see required tax deductions as follows:

Federal Tax – tax paid to the Internal Revenue Service on money earned. The federal tax above is $108.10

Carolyn Goodwin, CPA PLLC ©

Federal Insurance Contributions Act (FICA) for Medicare & Social Security - a tax collected by the federal government from those working that is placed into social security and Medicare accounts. This is a program to provide benefits (money) to people that are retired, disabled, and for children of deceased workers. This tax rate is 15.3%. The employee pays in half (7.65%) and the employer pays in half (7.65%) of this percentage. The employee's portion consists of 6.2% for social security and 1.45% for Medicare for a total of 7.65% and this must be deducted from each check based on the gross income earned. In this case $800. It is calculated as follows:

Gross Pay		$ 800.00	
FICA - Medicare	$800 X .0145	11.60	1.45%
FICA - Social Security	$800 X .062	49.60	6.20%
Total FICA tax paid by employee		61.20	7.65%
****Net Pay (Take home Check before state and federal deductions)**		$ 738.80	
** This does not take into account any other payroll deductions			
such as retirement; or state and federal taxes, etc.			

Business owners that are sole proprietors will pay this tax of 15.3% on their personal tax return. They do get a deduction for half (7.65%) of this tax, but it is not dollar for dollar. It only decreases their adjusted gross income they are reporting with the IRS.

State Tax - tax paid to the state you live in on money earned. (There could also be local tax based on where you live within your state). On this sample earning statement it is $40.

Since FICA tax is a standard rate (15.3% with the employer paying 7.65% and the employee paying 7.65%), you may be wondering how we know how much federal tax and state tax must be deducted from an employee's pay. When you have a job as an employee, you are required to fill out a from entitled 'W-4' to determine your federal tax and a state form depending on which state you are in. In this case, the state of NC uses form NC-4. See both forms on the following pages. After your employer (the organization or company that has hired you) receives these forms, they take the information to determine how much in taxes you will need to have deducted out of your check based on the information you provided.

Carolyn Goodwin, CPA PLLC ©

Form **W-4**

Department of the Treasury
Internal Revenue Service

Employee's Withholding Certificate

▶ Complete Form W-4 so that your employer can withhold the correct federal income tax from your pay.
▶ Give Form W-4 to your employer.
▶ Your withholding is subject to review by the IRS.

OMB No. 1545-0074

2020

Step 1: Enter Personal Information

(a) First name and middle initial | Last name | (b) Social security number

Address

City or town, state, and ZIP code

▶ Does your name match the name on your social security card? If not, to ensure you get credit for your earnings, contact SSA at 800-772-1213 or go to www.ssa.gov.

(c) ☐ **Single or Married filing separately**
☐ **Married filing jointly** (or Qualifying widow(er))
☐ **Head of household** (Check only if you're unmarried and pay more than half the costs of keeping up a home for yourself and a qualifying individual.)

Complete Steps 2–4 ONLY if they apply to you; otherwise, skip to Step 5. See page 2 for more information on each step, who can claim exemption from withholding, when to use the online estimator, and privacy.

Step 2: Multiple Jobs or Spouse Works

Complete this step if you (1) hold more than one job at a time, or (2) are married filing jointly and your spouse also works. The correct amount of withholding depends on income earned from all of these jobs.

Do **only one** of the following.

(a) Use the estimator at *www.irs.gov/W4App* for most accurate withholding for this step (and Steps 3–4); **or**

(b) Use the Multiple Jobs Worksheet on page 3 and enter the result in Step 4(c) below for roughly accurate withholding; **or**

(c) If there are only two jobs total, you may check this box. Do the same on Form W-4 for the other job. This option is accurate for jobs with similar pay; otherwise, more tax than necessary may be withheld . . . . . . ▶ ☐

TIP: To be accurate, submit a 2020 Form W-4 for all other jobs. If you (or your spouse) have self-employment income, including as an independent contractor, use the estimator.

Complete Steps 3–4(b) on Form W-4 for only ONE of these jobs. Leave those steps blank for the other jobs. (Your withholding will be most accurate if you complete Steps 3–4(b) on the Form W-4 for the highest paying job.)

Step 3: Claim Dependents

If your income will be $200,000 or less ($400,000 or less if married filing jointly):

Multiply the number of qualifying children under age 17 by $2,000 ▶ $ ________

Multiply the number of other dependents by $500 . . . . . ▶ $ ________

Add the amounts above and enter the total here . . . . **3** $

Step 4 (optional): Other Adjustments

(a) Other income (not from jobs). If you want tax withheld for other income you expect this year that won't have withholding, enter the amount of other income here. This may include interest, dividends, and retirement income . . . . **4(a)** $

(b) Deductions. If you expect to claim deductions other than the standard deduction and want to reduce your withholding, use the Deductions Worksheet on page 3 and enter the result here . . . . **4(b)** $

(c) Extra withholding. Enter any additional tax you want withheld each **pay period** . **4(c)** $

Step 5: Sign Here

Under penalties of perjury, I declare that this certificate, to the best of my knowledge and belief, is true, correct, and complete.

▶ **Employee's signature** (This form is not valid unless you sign it.) ▶ **Date**

Employers Only

Employer's name and address | First date of employment | Employer identification number (EIN)

For Privacy Act and Paperwork Reduction Act Notice, see page 3. Cat. No. 10220Q Form **W-4** (2020)

NCDOR
Web
11-19

NC-4
Employee's Withholding Allowance Certificate

PURPOSE - Complete Form NC-4 so that your employer can withhold the correct amount of State income tax from your pay. **If you do not provide an NC-4 to your employer, your employer is required to withhold based on the filing status, "Single" with zero allowances.**

FORM NC-4 EZ - You may use Form NC4-EZ if you plan to claim either the N.C. Standard Deduction or the N.C. Child Deduction Amount (but no other N.C. deductions), and you do not plan to claim any N.C. tax credits.

FORM NC-4 NRA - If you are a nonresident alien you must use Form NC-4 NRA. In general, a nonresident alien is an alien (not a U.S. citizen) who has not passed the green card test or the substantial presence test. *(See Publication 519, U.S. Tax Guide for Aliens, for more information on the green card test and the substantial presence test.)*

FORM NC-4 BASIC INSTRUCTIONS - Complete the NC-4 Allowance Worksheet. The worksheet will help you determine your withholding allowances based on federal and State adjustments to gross income including the N.C. Child Deduction Amount, N.C. itemized deductions, and N.C. tax credits. However, you may claim fewer allowances than you are entitled to if you wish to increase the tax withheld during the tax year. If your withholding allowances decrease, you must file a new NC-4 with your employer within 10 days after the change occurs. Exception: When an individual ceases to be "Head of Household" after maintaining the household for the major portion of the year, a new NC-4 is not required until the next year.

TWO OR MORE JOBS - If you have more than one job, determine the total number of allowances you are entitled to claim on all jobs using one Form NC-4 Allowance Worksheet. Your withholding will usually be most accurate when all allowances are claimed on the NC-4 filed for the higher paying job and zero allowances are claimed for the other. You should also refer to the "Multiple Jobs Table" to determine the additional amount to be withheld on Line 2 of Form NC-4 *(See page 4)*.

NONWAGE INCOME - If you have a large amount of nonwage income, such as interest or dividends, you should consider making estimated tax payments using Form NC-40 to avoid underpayment of estimated tax interest. Form NC-40 is available on the Department's website at www.ncdor.gov.

HEAD OF HOUSEHOLD - Generally you may claim "Head of Household" filing status on your tax return only if you are unmarried and pay more than 50% of the costs of keeping up a home for yourself and your dependent(s) or other qualifying individuals.

SURVIVING SPOUSE - You may claim "Surviving Spouse" filing status only if your spouse died in either of the two preceding tax years and you meet the following requirements:

1. Your home is maintained as the main household of a child or stepchild for whom you can claim a federal exemption; and
2. You were entitled to file a joint return with your spouse in the year of your spouse's death.

MARRIED TAXPAYERS - For married taxpayers, both spouses must agree as to whether they will complete the NC-4 Allowance Worksheet based on the filing status, "Married Filing Jointly" or "Married Filing Separately."

- Married taxpayers who complete the worksheet based on the filing status, "Married Filing Jointly" should consider the sum of both spouses' income, federal and State adjustments to income, and State tax credits to determine the number of allowances.
- Married taxpayers who complete the worksheet based on the filing status, "Married Filing Separately" should consider only his or her portion of income, federal and State adjustments to income, and State tax credits to determine the number of allowances.

All NC-4 forms are subject to review by the North Carolina Department of Revenue. Your employer may be required to send this form to the North Carolina Department of Revenue.

CAUTION: If you furnish an employer with an Employee's Withholding Allowance Certificate that contains information which has no reasonable basis and results in a lesser amount of tax being withheld than would have been withheld had you furnished reasonable information, you are subject to a penalty of 50% of the amount not properly withheld.

Cut here and give this certificate to your employer. Keep the top portion for your records.

NCDOR
Web
10-17

NC-4
Employee's Withholding Allowance Certificate

1. **Total number of allowances you are claiming**
   (Enter zero (0), or the number of allowances from Page 2, Line 17 of the NC-4 Allowance Worksheet) ____
2. **Additional amount, if any, withheld from each pay period** *(Enter whole dollars)* ________.00

Social Security Number ___ – __ – ____

Filing Status
☐ Single or Married Filing Separately ☐ Head of Household ☐ Married Filing Jointly or Surviving Spouse

First Name *(USE CAPITAL LETTERS FOR YOUR NAME AND ADDRESS)* ________ M.I. ___ Last Name ________

Address ________ County *(Enter first five letters)* ________

City ________ State ____ Zip Code (5 Digit) ________ Country *(If not U.S.)* ________

Employee's Signature ______________________ Date ____________

I certify, under penalties provided by law, that I am entitled to the number of withholding allowances claimed on Line 1 above.

Two taxes that will not be deducted but are paid by the employer on your behalf is Federal and State Unemployment. Most employers are taxed and must pay both taxes for each employee. These are payments that are set aside for workers who have lost their job. If your job is lost by no fault of your own, you can apply to receive unemployment funds until a job is found. For example, in a **recession** (a decline in economic activity, which can lead to businesses closing) the number of people losing their job increases because the business must cut back on its expenses. When this happens, more people are out of work and are applying for unemployment.

The amount of federal and state income taxes that has been deducted from your check is important because when you file your tax return each year you will need to report this to the Internal Revenue Service (IRS for short). The IRS is part of the Federal government of the United States. It's responsibility is to collect tax and make sure tax laws are followed. The agency decides how much tax is owed and collects revenue on a regular basis. For individuals, we pay our taxes throughout the year and on April 15th of the following year we fill out a form (1040) to send to the IRS. This shows how much money we have made and any amounts of money we paid or amounts to reduce our income as stated in tax laws that will decrease the amount of money we need to report to the IRS. Whatever we have left after this is called **taxable income**. This is the amount of income on your tax return that the IRS will say you owe taxes on. Luckily, by taking money out all year we can report to the IRS that we have paid taxes already. Sometimes we overpay and receive a refund from the IRS or at other times people underpay and have to pay the IRS money for the prior year. An example of the 1040 tax form is on the next page.

Carolyn Goodwin, CPA PLLC ©

Form **1040** Department of the Treasury—Internal Revenue Service (99) **U.S. Individual Income Tax Return** **2019** OMB No. 1545-0074 IRS Use Only—Do not write or staple in this space.

Filing Status Check only one box. ☐ Single ☐ Married filing jointly ☐ Married filing separately (MFS) ☐ Head of household (HOH) ☐ Qualifying widow(er) (QW)

If you checked the MFS box, enter the name of spouse. If you checked the HOH or QW box, enter the child's name if the qualifying person is a child but not your dependent. ▶

Your first name and middle initial	Last name	**Your social security number**
If joint return, spouse's first name and middle initial	Last name	**Spouse's social security number**
Home address (number and street). If you have a P.O. box, see instructions.	Apt. no.	**Presidential Election Campaign** Check here if you, or your spouse if filing jointly, want $3 to go to this fund. Checking a box below will not change your tax or refund. ☐ You ☐ Spouse
City, town or post office, state, and ZIP code. If you have a foreign address, also complete spaces below (see instructions).		
Foreign country name / Foreign province/state/county	Foreign postal code	If more than four dependents, see instructions and ✓ here ▶ ☐

Standard Deduction **Someone can claim:** ☐ You as a dependent ☐ Your spouse as a dependent
☐ Spouse itemizes on a separate return or you were a dual-status alien

Age/Blindness **You:** ☐ Were born before January 2, 1955 ☐ Are blind **Spouse:** ☐ Was born before January 2, 1955 ☐ Is blind

Dependents (see instructions): (1) First name	Last name	(2) Social security number	(3) Relationship to you	(4) ✓ if qualifies for (see instructions): Child tax credit	Credit for other dependents
				☐	☐
				☐	☐
				☐	☐
				☐	☐

Standard Deduction for—
- Single or Married filing separately, $12,200
- Married filing jointly or Qualifying widow(er), $24,400
- Head of household, $18,350
- If you checked any box under *Standard Deduction*, see instructions.

1	Wages, salaries, tips, etc. Attach Form(s) W-2				1	
2a	Tax-exempt interest	2a		b Taxable interest. Attach Sch. B if required	2b	
3a	Qualified dividends	3a		b Ordinary dividends. Attach Sch. B if required	3b	
4a	IRA distributions	4a		b Taxable amount	4b	
c	Pensions and annuities	4c		d Taxable amount	4d	
5a	Social security benefits	5a		b Taxable amount	5b	
6	Capital gain or (loss). Attach Schedule D if required. If not required, check here ▶ ☐				6	
7a	Other income from Schedule 1, line 9				7a	
b	Add lines 1, 2b, 3b, 4b, 4d, 5b, 6, and 7a. This is your **total income** ▶				7b	
8a	Adjustments to income from Schedule 1, line 22				8a	
b	Subtract line 8a from line 7b. This is your **adjusted gross income** ▶				8b	
9	**Standard deduction or itemized deductions** (from Schedule A)	9				
10	Qualified business income deduction. Attach Form 8995 or Form 8995-A	10				
11a	Add lines 9 and 10				11a	
b	**Taxable income.** Subtract line 11a from line 8b. If zero or less, enter -0-				11b	

For Disclosure, Privacy Act, and Paperwork Reduction Act Notice, see separate instructions. Cat. No. 11320B Form **1040** (2019)

Form 1040 (2019) Page 2

12a	Tax (see inst.) Check if any from Form(s): 1 ☐ 8814 2 ☐ 4972 3 ☐ ______	12a		
b	Add Schedule 2, line 3, and line 12a and enter the total ▶		12b	
13a	Child tax credit or credit for other dependents	13a		
b	Add Schedule 3, line 7, and line 13a and enter the total ▶		13b	
14	Subtract line 13b from line 12b. If zero or less, enter -0-		14	
15	Other taxes, including self-employment tax, from Schedule 2, line 10		15	
16	Add lines 14 and 15. This is your **total tax** ▶		16	
17	Federal income tax withheld from Forms W-2 and 1099		17	
18	Other payments and refundable credits:			
a	Earned income credit (EIC)	18a		
b	Additional child tax credit. Attach Schedule 8812	18b		
c	American opportunity credit from Form 8863, line 8	18c		
d	Schedule 3, line 14	18d		
e	Add lines 18a through 18d. These are your **total other payments and refundable credits** ▶		18e	
19	Add lines 17 and 18e. These are your **total payments** ▶		19	

• If you have a qualifying child, attach Sch. EIC.
• If you have nontaxable combat pay, see instructions.

Refund

Direct deposit? See instructions.

20	If line 19 is more than line 16, subtract line 16 from line 19. This is the amount you overpaid		20	
21a	Amount of line 20 you want **refunded to you.** If Form 8888 is attached, check here ▶ ☐		21a	
▶ b	Routing number ▶ c Type: ☐ Checking ☐ Savings			
▶ d	Account number			
22	Amount of line 20 you want **applied to your 2020 estimated tax** ▶	22		

Amount You Owe

23	**Amount you owe.** Subtract line 19 from line 16. For details on how to pay, see instructions ▶		23	
24	Estimated tax penalty (see instructions) ▶	24		

Third Party Designee
(Other than paid preparer)

Do you want to allow another person (other than your paid preparer) to discuss this return with the IRS? See instructions. ☐ **Yes. Complete below.** ☐ **No**

Designee's name ▶ Phone no. ▶ Personal identification number (PIN) ▶

Sign Here

Joint return? See instructions. Keep a copy for your records.

Under penalties of perjury, I declare that I have examined this return and accompanying schedules and statements, and to the best of my knowledge and belief, they are true, correct, and complete. Declaration of preparer (other than taxpayer) is based on all information of which preparer has any knowledge.

Your signature	Date	Your occupation	If the IRS sent you an Identity Protection PIN, enter it here (see inst.)
Spouse's signature. If a joint return, **both** must sign.	Date	Spouse's occupation	If the IRS sent your spouse an Identity Protection PIN, enter it here (see inst.)
Phone no.	Email address		

Paid Preparer Use Only

Preparer's name	Preparer's signature	Date	PTIN	Check if: ☐ 3rd Party Designee ☐ Self-employed
Firm's name ▶		Phone no.		
Firm's address ▶			Firm's EIN ▶	

Go to *www.irs.gov/Form1040* for instructions and the latest information. Form **1040** (2019)

Carolyn Goodwin, CPA PLLC ©

YOUR CALL TO ACTION

- Go to the Occupational Outlook Handbook on the web at https://www.bls.gov/ooh/. Include in your project a possible fringe benefit package that may be attached to compensation for your job/career of choice to research. Explain what fringe benefits would be important for you in deciding to accept an offer from a company or not.

Carolyn Goodwin, CPA PLLC ©

LESSON EXTENSION

Paycheck Calculation

Calculate the FICA – Medicare and social security tax on a paycheck that has a gross pay of $1,500. Remember – the total tax is 7.65%.

Note: we will not calculate the state tax at this time. Also, see if you can calculate and match your answer to the FICA tax shown on the paycheck in this chapter.

Carolyn Goodwin, CPA PLLC ©

Lesson 3

Financial Goals and Values

"Suppose one of you wants to build a tower. Won't you first sit down and estimate the cost to see if you have enough money to complete it?" Luke 14:28 (NIV)

Now that you have established a career and making money, now what? That is what the next question may be after receiving your first check. One of the first things to do is to have a plan…a financial plan before spending any of your money. Just as Luke 14:28 encourages a plan, we are to be vigilant about how we use the money God has put us stewards over. Before we move to the plan let's look at some vocabulary you'll need to know.

Vocabulary Words to Know

- **Needs** are goods or services that are required. Some examples are clothes, food, and shelter.

- **Wants** are goods or services that are not necessary, but that we wish or desire for. Some examples would be a television, tickets to a game, or a game station.

Okay, let's dig into the financial plan. Just as we would plan our day or our career path, we need to plan our finances. Planning will help us overcome obstacles that may prevent us from reaching our financial goals. If you are unsure of what your financial goals are it is a good exercise to write down your financial values to establish your financial goals. Also, there are time durations attached to financial goals. There are short term goals (goals that can be reached quickly) and long-term goals (goals that take longer to reach).

Carolyn Goodwin, CPA PLLC ©

Financial values are what something is worth as compared to something else, while financial goals are the desired results of your financial value. For example, something you may place a financial value on is your education. You may need supplies, money for class registration fees, or books. The financial goal would be receiving a college degree. The impact would be you would have to save up for your education instead of buying other things such as a car you would like to have. This would be a long-term goal for some and a short-term goal for others. For those in which it is short term this would be a major priority but for those in which it is long term, it may not be as big as a priority although it is one. The goal is important to prioritize because you will get the education you need to begin your career. Another value you may have is a desire to provide money to your parents. The financial goal would be to buy your parents a new home. The impact of buying a home for your parents may be you will have to use that money to buy your parents a home instead of buying a vacation home for yourself. Depending upon your urgency, this could be short-term or long-term. It would become a priority based on the time duration of the goal. How soon would you want to be able to buy your parents a home?

YOUR CALL TO ACTION

- Look at the list of expenses and circle if each is a need or a want.

Apartment Rent - $1,000	Need / Want
Groceries - $150	Need / Want
Eating Out - $100	Need / Want
Renter's Insurance - $12	Need / Want
Utilities (gas, electric, water) - $100	Need / Want
Cable - $50	Need / Want
Internet - $50	Need / Want
Pet care (food, litter, etc.) - $40	Need / Want

⊙ Calculate the cost of saving for 3 financial goals. What is the impact of saving for these goals and how should you prioritize these goals? Why is it important to prioritize?

1) Goal: ______________________________

Impact: ______________________________

____

How should I prioritize my goal? Is my goal short-term or long-term?

____

____

Why is it important to prioritize my goal?

____

Carolyn Goodwin, CPA PLLC ©

2) Goal: ____

Impact:____

How should I prioritize my goal? Is my goal short-term or long-term?

Why is it important to prioritize my goal?

3) Goal: ____

Impact:____

Carolyn Goodwin, CPA PLLC ©

How should I prioritize my goal? Is my goal short-term or long-term?

____

____

Why is it important to prioritize my goal?

____

____

LESSON EXTENSION

Carolyn Goodwin, CPA PLLC ©

As you determine your short-term goals, establish a plan for how you will obtain income to reach those goals. You may have something small or something big you would like to purchase. How will you go about making money? Do you have a job already? You could talk to your parents or guardians about doing chores to help around the house and/or you have a business idea in which you can sell products or services. We will discuss budgeting once there is a source of income in the next chapter.

Carolyn Goodwin, CPA PLLC ©

Lesson 4

Personal Budgeting

"On the first day of every week, each one of you should set aside a sum of money in keeping with your income, saving it up, so that when I come no collections will have to be made." I Corinthians 16:2 (NIV)

Now that we have clear financial goals and values, we can make decisions about what to do with our money. We should plan out where our money is going before we get paid. This process is called budgeting. A budget is an estimate of your income (money earned) and expenses (money to be paid out). A personal budget is for your household. We use it as a tool to map out our financial plan. Budgets can be written down on paper, put into a spreadsheet, or used in a budgeting software or app. To make a budget, you don't have to do anything sophisticated. Do whatever you are comfortable with…just make sure you have one! Proverbs 27:12 reads, "A sensible man watches for problems ahead and *prepares* to meet them. The simpleton never looks and suffers the consequences." If we never plan and look ahead at what we will do with our money when we get it there will be consequences of mismanagement of the money we have. This will result in a lack of money to cover expenses that are important and necessary for day-to-day living.

The most important part of a budget is to make sure your expenses do not exceed your income. When this happens, you have a deficit. There is not enough income to cover your expenses. There are 2 kinds of expenses we are going to have in our budget. They are **fixed expenses** and **variable expenses**. A **fixed expense** is a cost you have that will remain the same. An example of fixed expenses may be your car payment or a monthly magazine subscription. A **variable expense** is a cost that changes over time. These costs could be gas for your car, clothing, or entertainment.

There are 3 things we do with our money. We will explore more in the following chapters.

- Give
- Save
- Spend

Carolyn Goodwin, CPA PLLC ©

YOUR CALL TO ACTION

- Look at the list of expenses from the previous chapter that are listed below. Go through the expenses and determine if these are fixed or variable expenses based on the definition and examples given.

Apartment Rent - $1,000	Fixed / Variable
Groceries - $150	Fixed / Variable
Eating Out - $100	Fixed / Variable
Renter's Insurance - $12	Fixed / Variable
Utilities (gas, electric, water) - $100	Fixed / Variable
Cable - $50	Fixed / Variable
Internet - $50	Fixed / Variable
Pet care (food, litter, etc.) - $40	Fixed / Variable

LESSON EXTENSION

- Come up with some of your own fixed and variable expenses you may need for your budget in the next chapter.

Carolyn Goodwin, CPA PLLC ©

Lesson 5

Managing your Money – Give, Save, Spend

"Go to the ant, sluggard: consider her ways and be wise; who, having no guide, overseer, or ruler, provides her food in the summer and gathers her food in the harvest." Proverbs 6: 6-8

When we give, we give to help others and/or to further the mission or purpose of places of worship and/or other organizations. Giving may be done by tithes (setting aside a specific amount of money to give on a regular basis) and/or offering at our places of worship or other donations to charitable organizations. Giving to our places of worship can help with outreach programs to help others. More importantly, giving to your place of worship helps with the upkeep and maintenance of the building. A **charitable organization** is an organization setup to help those in need. For example, if you have a strong desire to help those that are homeless you can help by giving a portion of your income to an organization with a mission to help those that have no place to live. There are other ways to give, such as your time. Since this book is specifically about financial responsibility, we will remain focused on giving financially as a part of our budgeting process.

One of the most important things to do with your money is to pay yourself first. You can start by setting up an emergency fund for unexpected costs of at least $1,000. We should look to begin saving at least 10% of our money we earn for a "rainy day" into our emergency fund. Your rainy day may be an unexpected bill such as a car or home repair.

This is a rainy day because what has happened is not part of your budget. There is nothing worse than having your budget all prepared and having an unexpected bill arise.

When we save, we are preparing and planning for the future. An expense may be unexpected, and we need to have a reserve (savings) set aside for that. Therefore, you will not have to borrow money to take care of your expenses. Think about age old parable of the grasshopper and the ant. The ant works hard in the summer to store up for the winter. God created some business-minded insects when he created them! They prepare and plan for the hard times during the winter. The grasshopper, on the other hand, spends leisure time and have fun during the summer collecting no food only to find he is without when winter comes. The same thing applies to us. We do not want to be the grasshopper in this story of life!

After funding your emergency fund, save 10% - 15% of your earnings that goes to your savings account, investment account, or retirement account. You can even have this money deposited to your accounts automatically as you get paid and you do not have to remember to do it manually. In addition, you will have the added advantage of growing your money starting at an early age. The sooner you save, the more money you will have for later. So, start early!

A way you can save money is by opening a **savings account** or a **money market** account. Some accounts pay interest, but money market accounts normally pay more interest than a savings account. These accounts are used to deposit (add money into) money that you do not plan to use immediately. You can have money taken out of or deducted from your check automatically through your regular check just like the deductions we reviewed in Lesson 2 or you can take your deposit to the bank using a deposit slip or ATM (automated teller machine). Deposit slips look different from bank to bank but will require the same information to make a deposit. Here, you will find an example of a deposit slip.

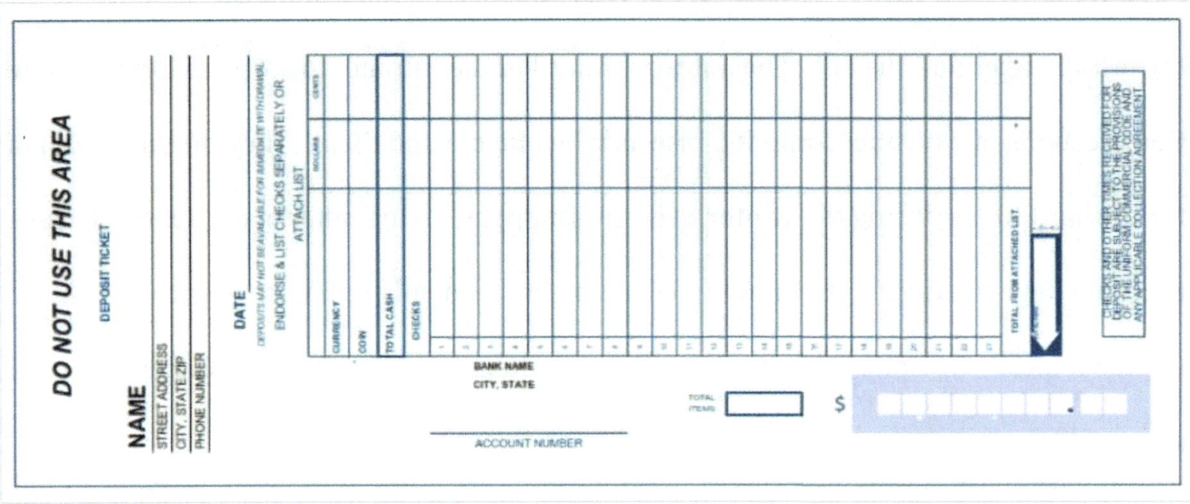

Another option is a **certificate of deposit (CD)** which is like a savings account and is guaranteed from loss by the bank. The difference between a regular account and a CD is you are encouraged to leave the money with the bank for a certain amount of time with the CD. If you take your money out before that time, you may have to pay a penalty (an order to pay) for using it before the time allowed.

Take note that you can deposit money into a checking or savings account. If you do not have expenses to pay, put your money into a savings account. Oftentimes, the bank may pay **interest.** Interest is money paid regularly at a specific rate because the bank is using your money. It is a percentage that is set by the **Federal Reserve.** The **Federal Reserve** is the central bank in the United States. It was founded in 1913 and oversees the amount of money in circulation and interest rates. In addition, this agency is basically the bank bankers go to just like regular citizens go to the bank. When banks get into trouble, the **Federal Reserve** loans money to the bank to keep it from going out of business.

As it relates to your savings, we can have **compound interest**. The higher the interest rate the greater the amount that can be saved. There are 3 definitions that are useful in figuring out compound interest. The **principal, interest, and compounding. Principal** is the amount of money you deposit originally. **Interest** is the money earned from your deposit. **Compounding** is interest both on principal and the previously earned interest. Interest is earned on the money you put in, plus on the money the bank put in as interest. For example, if you invest $100 and your interest rate is 3% ($100 x .03), then you will have $103.00. The next time interest is paid out you will be paid on the $103.00 ($103.00 x .03) which means you will have $106.09. You will earn interest on the principal ($100) and interest you previously earned ($3.00).

What if the bank fails after I give them my money? What will happen to all the money deposited? When you go to make your deposit, take note that there is a FDIC logo on the door or in the window at the bank. This stands for **Federal Deposit Insurance Corporation (FDIC)**. This is a government corporation that provides **insurance** (a guarantee of protection if anyone experience loss or damage) to those making deposits to commercial banks and savings institutions in the United States. If you are depositing into a credit union, your money is protected by the **National Credit Union Administration**

Carolyn Goodwin, CPA PLLC ©

(NCUA). This protection was created in 1933 as part of the Banking Act during the Great Depression so that people will trust the banks again. Other government agencies that protect the safety of customers and enforce compliance are the Consumer Financial Protection Bureau (helps protect consumers by making sure companies are fair and don't manipulate or take advantage of consumers), the Office of the Comptroller of Currency (regulates national, foreign, and federal banks), and state banking departments.

Another way to pay yourself first is through retirement savings. As discussed in the prior chapter, retirement contributions and accounts can be set up through an employer but can also be established without an employer. Business owners have the same opportunity to establish retirement accounts. Some IRAs that are available are:

- **Traditional IRA** – an individual retirement account in which contributions are made pre-tax. The owner will pay tax only when they are able to withdraw funds after they turn 59 ½.
- **Roth IRA** - an individual retirement account in which contributions are made after-tax. This account is tax free which means you do not have to pay taxes on any money you take out of the account as long as the account has been opened for five (5) years and you are age 59 ½ or older.
- **Education savings account** – established within your state of residence. Funds are set aside to assist families in funding educational expenses.

Carolyn Goodwin, CPA PLLC ©

After giving and saving, we are left with our spending money that we can use to pay bills and purchase items we need or want. When it comes to spending, there are a couple of things we spend money on. We spend based on ***needs*** and ***wants***. A ***need*** is something you must have, and a ***want*** is something you would like to have. You truly only need a few things to survive in our current day - shelter, food and water, healthcare and hygiene products, and clothing (enough to be comfortable and dressed appropriately). Anything else beyond that is a want. There are a few things we could make an exception for based on the day and age we are in. For example, we could say you would need a car or want a car based on your circumstances and if you have access public transportation. We may need internet to work but not so much for leisurely browsing.

This process may sound a little backwards but if this is the order in which you make a part of your life at an early age (give, save, and then spend), you will not think twice about the money you give and save before you spend. Remember, all that we have belongs to God. You will find that there are several testimonies from people that were faithful to give and God always made a way for them and provided more. "Give, and it will be given to you. They will pour into your lap a good measure pressed down, shaken together, and running over. For by your standard of measure it will be measured to you in return." Luke 6:38. In summary, this means that when we give, blessings will be poured out to us and overflow because of our faithfulness. Those blessings are not always financially but in other ways. Now let's not think that we will give just to receive. We must give with good intent, not just with an expectation to receive something in return.

One tip to save money for all areas of giving, saving, and spending is to use the envelope method. This means you take 3 envelopes and label them give, save, spend. When you receive money split the money up into the percentages or portions you have allocated for each envelope. For example, you get $100 for your birthday. You will take 10% or $10 and put that in your giving envelope, 10% or $10 into your savings, and the remainder ($80) into the spend envelope.

Ways to save more are:

- Never accumulate credit card debt. If you must use a credit card, always pay your balance off every month.
- Spend less than you make.
- Use the 4-week rule. Wait four weeks before you buy anything. This will decrease impulse buying (buying without thinking).
- Make sure you do not create bad money habits. Do not spend money on things you don't need such as coffee at cafes every day, subscriptions that aren't being used, gym memberships, and cable to name a few. Use your money wisely and find alternative ways to minimize these costs.
- Contribute to your 401(k) plan for retirement.
- Pack your lunch. Do not make it a habit to eat out every day. This adds up over time and that money could be saved or put towards a financial goal.

Carolyn Goodwin, CPA PLLC ©

Now, let's look at a budget. You will get an opportunity to put a budget together based on some numbers below.

Carolyn Goodwin, CPA PLLC ©

YOUR CALL TO ACTION

- Look at the list of expenses below. Write out your budget based on the information presented in this chapter. Make sure you are not left with a deficit. Your expenses should not be more than your income. Here are some questions to keep in mind. What are some things you really do not need and what are necessary? Remember, needs vs. wants? This matters when budgeting! Fixed expenses have been given. Determine how much you can afford to spend on variable expenses and establish your budget. Your income for the month is $2,500.

Income $2,500
Fixed Expenses:
Giving/donations
Save
Car Insurance - $80
Apartment Rent - $1,000
Renter's Insurance - $12
Utilities (gas, electric, water) - $100
Cable - $50
Internet - $50
Car Payment $250
Groceries
Eating Out
Clothing

My Budget

Carolyn Goodwin, CPA PLLC ©

- When you receive money, practice the envelope method.
- Go to the bank with your parent or guardian and learn about the different types of savings accounts. Most banks have quite a few and you must determine the one that will best suit your needs. Open an account while you are visiting.

Carolyn Goodwin, CPA PLLC ©

LESSON EXTENSION

- If you receive an allowance or get money for special occasions, use the personal budgeting process for giving, saving, and spending. If you start early, it will be something you will do without thinking for the rest of your life.
- Calculate the compound interest for the years indicated that can be received on the following savings accounts.
    - Savings account A – 3% interest paid annually over 3 years: $250 initial deposit
    - Savings account B – 2% interest paid annual over 5 years: $300 initial deposit
- The days of writing checks are slowly fading but it is important to be able to write a check and know how to read one if others are still using checks. Let's practice writing a check! Check your work compared to the answers in the back of the book. Lines to fill in:
    - Date – The date the check is written. Be sure to write your date as xx/xx/20xx.
    - Pay to the order of – The person or business you are writing the check out to.
    - $ box – The amount of money you are paying written in numbers. Example $250.$^{\underline{34}}$ Be sure to raise the cents. This will prevent anyone from manipulating your check by adding numbers and deleting decimals.
    - "Dollars" line – handwritten dollar amount of the check. Example: Two-hundred fifty dollars and $\frac{34}{100}$ ____________________. Carry the dash out to the 'dollars' word so nothing can be added to the words you have written by anyone else.

Carolyn Goodwin, CPA PLLC ©

- For – If you would like, you can reference what the check is for, an account number for which you are making payment on, or an invoice number .
- Signature line – your signature in cursive
- Note the check number in the upper right-hand corner. This is good for tracking your checks written.

- Now that you have written your check, how do we determine what your balance is in your checkbook? Let's learn to balance your checkbook based off of the numbers from 'Your Call to Action'. When you make a payment, sometimes the money is not drafted right away from your account. To avoid spending that money before it drafts (comes out) of your account, it is a good practice to "balance your checkbook". Even though most people do not use a checkbook anymore. Any method that will work for you can be used. A spreadsheet or an app you can find will suffice. We will base these numbers off your budgeted items in this chapter. Study and take note of the example to gain an understanding of how to do this.

Checkbook Register

Name: ____________________

Current Balance:	**1,396.00**
Cleared Balance:	1,646.00
Warn when balance is below:	500.00

See instructions in the Help worksheet

Date	Num	Payee / Descr	Category	Cleared - C	Withdrawal, Payment (-)	Deposit, Credit (+)	Balance
1/01/19		[Balance As of 01/01/2019]				546.00	546.00
1/01/19	DEP	Direct Deposit from Employer	Paycheck	c		2,500.00	3,046.00
1/10/19	EFT	Car Payment	Vehicle Payments		250.00		2,796.00
1/15/19	2032	Joe's Food Mart	Groceries	c	300.00		2,496.00
1/22/19	2033	Rent Payment	Mortgage/Rent	c	1,100.00		1,396.00

*Spreadsheet was adapted from Microsoft Excel

**Note the C is for items that have cleared or shown up on your bank account or statement. These can be checked off so that you will know the funds that have come out of your account. Note the vehicle payment has not cleared but you will know it will eventually draft out of your account. You can rest assured your balance of $1,396 is what you have in your account to spend and not $1,646 ($1,396 + $250).

- We will now practice filling out a deposit slip. You would need to fill in the following fields:
    - Date
    - Your Name
    - Address
    - Account number

- Cash or check amount you will deposit, cash you will keep (if applicable and if you are cashing a check)

Carolyn Goodwin, CPA PLLC ©

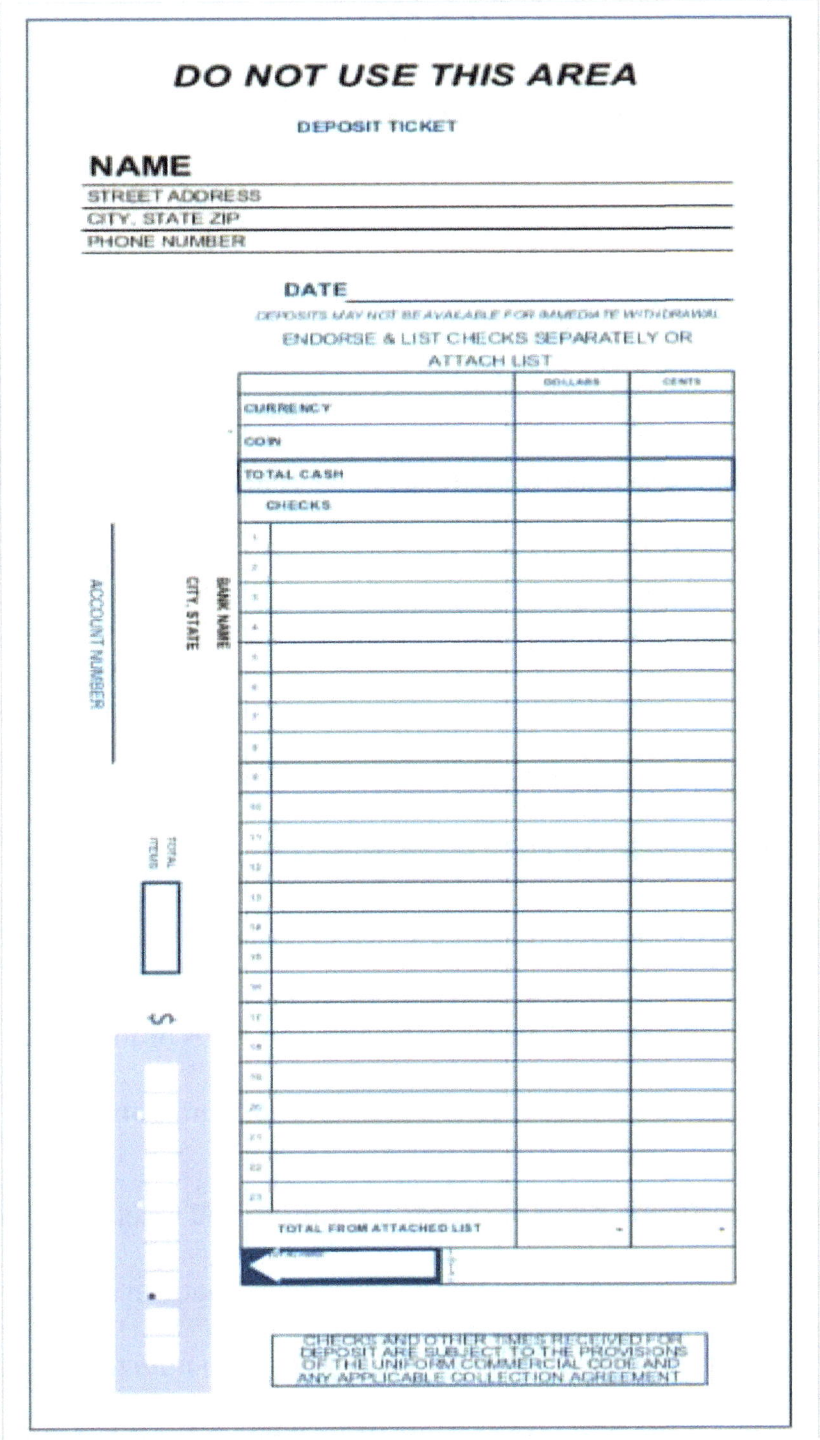

DO NOT USE THIS AREA

DEPOSIT TICKET

NAME
STREET ADDRESS
CITY, STATE ZIP
PHONE NUMBER

DATE ______

DEPOSITS MAY NOT BE AVAILABLE FOR IMMEDIATE WITHDRAWAL

ENDORSE & LIST CHECKS SEPARATELY OR ATTACH LIST

	DOLLARS	CENTS
CURRENCY		
COIN		
TOTAL CASH		
CHECKS		
1		
2		
3		
4		
5		
6		
7		
8		
9		
10		
11		
12		
13		
14		
15		
16		
17		
18		
19		
20		
21		
22		
23		
TOTAL FROM ATTACHED LIST	-	-

BANK NAME
CITY, STATE
ACCOUNT NUMBER
TOTAL ITEMS
$

CHECKS AND OTHER TIMES RECEIVED FOR DEPOSIT ARE SUBJECT TO THE PROVISIONS OF THE UNIFORM COMMERCIAL CODE AND ANY APPLICABLE COLLECTION AGREEMENT

Carolyn Goodwin, CPA PLLC ©

Lesson 6

Invest! Growing Money

"The plans of the diligent lead surely to advantage, but everyone who is hasty comes surely to poverty." Proverbs 21: 5

Investing is the process of committing money to an endeavor expecting a profit, although it is not guaranteed. People invest in several different ways and build an **investment portfolio** (a collection of all your **financial assets** such as stocks, bonds, and cash). Investing without a guarantee of profit involves **risk.** Risk is the likelihood that you will lose money in what you have invested. It is a chance you take. You can increase your wealth over time, but with the risk of loss or an increase of reward. When there is a high risk in what you are investing in, the reward and the loss is often high as well. Investors must determine if they are comfortable with the risk they are looking to take.

Some different types of **investment vehicles** (the different ways or methods a person or business can use to invest money) are **stocks, mutual funds**, and **bonds.**

- A **stock** is an investment in which **shares** (certificate you receive) are owned of the assets and earnings of a company. It is an investment made in a business and you become partial owner of the company. It is important to note that the more popular a stock is more people will want to buy it. We call this **demand**. If there is a low **supply** (the amount available) this will move the price of the stock up. In the same way if the stock is in less demand, the price of the stock would decline.

Carolyn Goodwin, CPA PLLC ©

- A **mutual fund** is an investment tool that combines the money from shareholders and invests it in many securities such as stocks, bonds, or money markets.

- A **bond** is a loan note issued by the government or a corporation and sold to the public. You are agreeing to loan your money to these institutions, and they are promising they will pay you back what you have invested plus interest after an agreed upon time. The money you invest is used by governments or corporations to help them pay off debt or to carry out special projects.

- Real estate such as homes, buildings, and land are also considered investments.

Stocks are bought and sold at a **stock** market. The **New York Stock Exchange** is an example of one. It is the second largest stock exchange in the world. The NYSE is in New York City, New York. A stock may allow you to contribute to decision making as to how the company is run and other decisions that are to be made. You will become a **shareholder** in the company. **Shareholders** invest in companies to make a profit. Your investment can increase in value (**appreciation)** and you earn a **dividend** (money a company gives to its shareholders) when companies make a profit. This is known as a **capital gain.** If the company did not make a profit, there will be a decrease in value (**depreciation** of your stock) resulting in a **capital loss**. Stocks have more risk than savings bonds. Savings bonds, on the other hand, are much like a savings account that pays interest. Instead, savings bonds are bought and accumulate interest over years. They do not carry a high interest rate so the risk of investing in a bond is low. In a mutual fund you invest in small portions of various stocks, not just one. The stock mutual funds are less risky than

Carolyn Goodwin, CPA PLLC ©

individual stock investments because you are **diversifying** your investments. **Diversification** is a way to reduce your risk by investing in a variety of investments. You are spreading your money so you will not lose much if one company in your investment pool loses money. The phrase "not putting all of your eggs in one basket" can be used to describe **diversification.**

Over a period of owning a financial asset that you've invested in; an analysis is good to use to determine if the rate of return on your investment is worth keeping. As discussed, assets do not always hold their value. They can sometimes depreciate or appreciate. Therefore, a calculation of the **rate of return** is a valuable analysis. For example, let's say you buy a stock for $80 per share. You own this stock for 5 years and earn a dividend of $5. A **dividend** is money that the company you have invested in pays to its shareholders on a regular basis (usually every three months or quarterly). This dividend comes out of the company's profits (more income than expenses). If you sell the stock for $100, your gain will be $20. You also earned a dividend of $5 so your gain will be a total of $25. To determine the rate of return we divide the gain of $25 by the cost per share that was paid for the stock ($80) for a rate of return of 31% or 0.3125. That would be a rather good rate of return for what you invested.

Let's use a bond as an example. This calculation is a little different than that of a stock. There is a bond you purchased for $1,000. This bond is a $1,000 **par value** 5% **coupon bond**. Let's look at some terminology before moving on. **Par value** is the face value or the dollar amount you will receive from the issuer of the bond at **maturity** (the date the bondholder (you) receives the money back). A **coupon bond** is a bond that pays interest (annually, semiannually, or quarterly). This investment will be an annual coupon bond. The bond earns $50 for one year. If it is sold for $1,200 a gain of $200 would be recognized along with $50 in interest. Again, the gain is divided by the cost to determine the rate of return. The rate of return would be calculated as follows: $200 + 50 = $250 gain; divide $250 by $1,000 = 25% rate of return or 0.2500. This bond was sold at a **premium** (an amount above face or par value). If it was sold below the face or par value we call that a **discount**.

We see in both examples the value of the stock and bond appreciated over time and you as the investor was able to recognize a capital gain. It is wise to factor in costs such as taxes and investment fees into the rate of return calculation, if possible. These costs would decrease the gain recognized.

Carolyn Goodwin, CPA PLLC ©

YOUR CALL TO ACTION

- Look at the list of investments. Determine if the investment is lower risk or higher risk.

Money market account	Lower Risk / Higher Risk
Savings account	Lower Risk / Higher Risk
Mutual fund	Lower Risk / Higher Risk
Stocks	Lower Risk / Higher Risk
Certificate of deposit	Lower Risk / Higher Risk

- Calculate the rate of return on the following financial assets:

    - Bond - $1000 par value 5% coupon bond issuing coupon payments annually. The bond is sold for $1500. Is it sold at a premium or a discount?

    - Stock at $50 per share. Five shares are purchased. Dividend of 10% is paid over 5 years. The stock is sold for $500.

- Research and find a company that you would like to invest in. This company must be publicly traded on the stock market. Track the stock for this company over 2 weeks. Use the tracking sheet on the following page to record the progress.

LESSON EXTENSION

- After tracking your stock for 2 weeks, is this a stock you would like to invest in? Is there another stock you would like to invest in? Instead of spending all your allowance, special occasion money, or paycheck challenge yourself instead to invest in a stock. Several options are available for anyone under age 18 to invest in stock with parental oversight.

Carolyn Goodwin, CPA PLLC ©

Lesson 7

Let's Shop ! Be a Smart, Savvy Shopper

"So if you have not been trustworthy in handling worldly wealth, who will trust you with true riches?" Luke 16:11

At some point in life, there will be items that we have our eye on that we want and cannot wait to get our hands on. Thoughts are racing as to how you can get that item you want so badly. With a budget laid out, you are on your way to make your much-anticipated purchase. How do you strategize how you will make the purchase, where you purchase it from, and/or how to compare prices? Before running off to get the first thing you see, it is a good idea to think your purchase through before you buy. Will this be an item that you will be able to use and get your money's worth out of or will it be that item you get from the $1 section and end up putting it away or throwing it away after it breaks?!

When you get a commission, special occasion money, such as from a birthday, or paycheck, immediately spending what you have is a habit that you do not want to start. We all know that phones can be expensive. Let's say you have your eye on a new phone that you need or just want. Your old one is working fine though. This will require saving your money to make this expensive purchase. Instead of going to the store to get the newest and most expensive shoes you decide to delay that purchase to buy what you have been wanting all this time. This is called **delayed**

Carolyn Goodwin, CPA PLLC ©

gratification. As the old saying goes "we can't have our cake and eat it too." We must choose which purchase will be more beneficial in the long term.

You do not have to have a process to think through if you need to purchase a pencil for math class but having a process to think through large purchases is important. Below is a list of things to think about before you make a purchase.

1) *Determine if what you are getting is a need or a want.* Is this something you really need or something you can do without? If you can do without it, you should continue saving your money. There may be something that you find you really want but you do not have the money for it.

2) *Why do you want this item?* List out 3 reasons.

3) *Let's compare the prices from several different stores or online and choose 2-3 as your final decisions.* Where can I get this item cheaper? Sometimes stores have cheaper prices and sometimes there are online deals, and the prices are cheaper. Do not buy from the first retailer you see. Check advertisements from retailers. An **advertisement** is a notice or announcement in a public medium promoting a product, service, or event or publicizing a job vacancy. Are the advertising tactics influencing you to purchase one item over the other?

4) *Look at the features.* Is there another item that is the same but just a different **brand name** that you could possibly get that is cheaper?

Carolyn Goodwin, CPA PLLC ©

5) *Ask your parents or guardians if they have coupons or any deals that have come through their email or mail.* Oftentimes, adults sign up for a lot of rewards and get coupons all the time. If you find a coupon, determine how much you will be able to save using it and compare it to other places you are looking to buy from. Sometimes using the coupon at one store does not make a difference because another store may have the product at a lower cost than what you would pay with the coupon. Math at work on this one! Unless your parent approves of you signing up for rewards, it is a great idea to ask around in your family.

6) *Look at the **opportunity cost**.* **Opportunity cost** is the value of possible alternatives that a person gives up when making one choice instead of another, also known as a trade-off. For example, the opportunity cost of buying a car is the money you would save taking the bus to work instead. On the other hand, the cost of riding the bus could be cheaper and money could be saved.

7) *If you have gone through your list and feel good about the information you gathered ask yourself how this will affect your spending budget.*

Carolyn Goodwin, CPA PLLC ©

YOUR CALL TO ACTION

- Choose an item you would like to purchase and gather your information such as price, deals and coupons, name brand, features, and opportunity cost on the sheet attached. If there is not anything you would like to purchase now, choose something you may be interested in.

Item I would like to purchase:____

Is this item a need or a want? ____________________________________

Why do I want to purchase this item?

____

Compare the prices from several different stores or online and choose 2-3 as your final decisions. Look at the features. Is there another item that is the same but just a different **brand name** that you could possibly get that is cheaper?

Option 1	Option 2	Option 3

Coupons or deals I have found:

Opportunity Costs

Carolyn Goodwin, CPA PLLC ©

How will this affect my spending budget?

____

____

LESSON EXTENSION

- Get approval for the purchase from your parent or guardian. Sit down with your parent or guardian and determine the best way to purchase (online or at the store).

Carolyn Goodwin, CPA PLLC ©

Lesson 8

Credit & Debt Smarts

"Just as the rich rule the poor, so the borrower is servant to the lender."
Proverbs 21:5

Two of the most common types of credit are **installment loans** and **revolving credit**. **Installment loans** are a set amount of money that is lent to you for a specific purpose. They could be student loans, auto loans, or mortgage loans. **Revolving credit** is a line of credit you can keep using even after you pay it off. What you purchase must stay under the **credit limit** (the amount a lender approves of you to borrow, although it could change over time). Credit cards are the most common. A **credit card** is much different from a **debit card**. A **debit card** is a plastic card that has *your* money attached to it. It is only what you have in the bank. It is ***not*** a loan. A **credit card** is a plastic card that is used to purchase goods and services in exchange for future payment with **interest** (a percentage of your purchases the lender will charge in addition to what you have purchased; this makes it worth their time to extend a loan to you and is also a way for creditors to make money). Installment loans and revolving credit are all considered **debt** (money owed).

There may be times in life that we have an item in mind that we want but do not have the cash to pay for it. It may be a home or a car. Other times people obtain student loans to attend college. There are times when a new outfit may grab your attention and you do not have the cash but rather reach for a credit card to make the purchase. Then we come to

Carolyn Goodwin, CPA PLLC ©

those emergencies when the cash is just not available, and the decision is made to apply for a loan or to use **credit.** In all these cases, it is a good idea to evaluate whether you really need the loan or credit. Not all credit is good and not all credit is bad. We can save or we can go through our step-by-step process in the previous chapter to evaluate whether the purchase is necessary. As it relates to education, we could opt to find all the scholarships we can or set up a payment plan to pay for school. It is important that we are wise about loans and credit we are willing to apply for and accept. For example, as college students transition into freshman year, there are credit card companies on campus that lure college students in to applying for a credit card in exchange for something free. Is it worth applying to get that credit card and using it to get free pizza or to buy a new outfit? Never! There is a lot more attached to credit card ownership.

Installment loans on the other hand is a set amount of money you must pay back. If you are receiving a loan for $1,000, the lender (bank, financial institution etc.) will have an interest rate that will be paid in addition to the **principal** (the amount borrowed). Banks and financial institutions loan funds from those that deposit money to borrowers. For example, if you make a deposit into your account at a bank, those funds are then used to loan to another individual that comes into the bank looking for funds. A payment amount is calculated to be paid on a set **term** (how often the payment is to be paid to the lender, normally monthly).

There are pros and cons to credit. Some pros of credit are convenience as they are accepted all over. There is security in knowing that if you lose your card, you can just cancel, whereas when cash is lost or stolen it is gone for good. You will have immediate access to money but be cautioned to use it wisely. Only use it when you can immediately pay off what you charge as not to incur interest. One feature companies use to encourage one to apply for and get credit cards is to offer rewards. The rewards are earned as you use your card. This can be free travel or your choice to choose gift cards or other items for the rewards you have accumulated. Again, instead of getting caught in the trap of using the card just for rewards it is wise to pay your card off immediately or forgo getting the card at all. Some cons to credit are the interest as discussed previously. There are also fees to have some credit cards such as an annual fee that is like a renewal fee each year to have the card. You will also have debt that may become overbearing to pay back. Overspending is another con as the card can feel like you are not using money at all and the charges can quickly get out of hand.

If you plan to apply for that credit card, it could come with a ridiculous **annual percentage rate (APR)** or it could end up being a ridiculous rate over time. An **annual percentage rate (APR)** is the fee you pay for borrowing money and is a reflection of how much interest you will pay The credit card company compound the interest you owe on the card daily. If you have a card with a 15% APR, you would divide that by 365 days in the year. The daily rate would be 0.041%. If you spent $1,000 on food and other things you needed for college and could not pay it off within the 21-day **grace period** (the period of time you have to pay the card completely off before being charged interest), you would multiply the $1,000 by the 0.041% daily rate for the first day. Your balance in that one day has gone up to $1,000.41. On the second day, you would take the $1,000.41 and multiply it again by

0.041% and you would have to pay back $1,000.82 and it continues to compound. If you compound this amount over 30 days, you will owe $1,012.50 instead of just the $1,000 you borrowed. Over a year you would owe $1,160.75. That is $160.75 extra you must pay in addition to purchases that have been made on the card. That does not consider new purchases along the way. Getting that card and not paying for the food and other items needed for college could really add up.

Credit is not a bad thing. It just needs to be used wisely and with caution. When leaving home and going off on your own, it is important to establish good credit. This will give you a better chance at obtaining a loan which includes a credit card. When applying for a loan or credit card you will more likely be offered low or reasonable interest rates which will save you money. When you apply for a job, insurance policies, or an apartment your credit history will be considered as well. If credit is bad there is a possibility you could pay more for insurance and if renting you could be denied or if it is approved there may be a larger security deposit required.

Some ways to build good credit are:

- Pay your amounts due for loans, bills, or other debts on time. This shows you are managing your finances responsibly.
- Pay off your credit card immediately. Try to charge only what you can afford to pay off immediately.

- Check your **credit report** often for errors. A **credit report** shows information about your credit such as some of your bill repayment history, the status of your credit accounts (how often you make your payments on time, how much credit you have available, how much of that credit you are using, and whether a debt or bill collector is collecting on money that is owed by you). The three major credit reporting agencies are Equifax, Experian, and TransUnion. There are smaller ones as well. They collect and maintain information about consumer credit and in turn sell it to other business in a consumer's credit report.

- Keep in mind if you have multiple inquiries on your credit report it can affect your credit negatively. Therefore, be careful of the number and type of accounts you decide to establish as new credit.

- If you are new to establishing credit, apply for a bank loan secured by funds you have on deposit.

- For teens, sometimes a parent may **cosign (a person agrees to share the liability for the loan with you)** for their children to get a loan or credit card if the parent has good enough credit. This will give the student an opportunity to establish credit.

- Make sure you understand the terms of the credit you are applying for.

Carolyn Goodwin, CPA PLLC ©

Lesson 9

How To Protect Your Identity

"They lie awake at night, hatching sinful plots...". Psalm 36:4

It is not hard to believe in the world we live in that there are people out there ready to take what we have and have worked so hard for. Imagine you have been saving up for a new phone that you needed desperately. You go to the store and accidentally leave it, and someone takes it. That is a bad feeling given you spent your time saving and that was the last of your spending money.

This is what happens with **identity theft** except this theft is purely for economic or financial gain. **Identity theft** is a crime. Someone normally uses another person's personal information such as their name, Social Security number, credit or debit card number, bank account number, or anything else that is personal. Your personal data can be taken and used for someone else's gain. Many people obtain another person's information to take money out of a bank account that does not belong to them and apply for credit in another person's name, for example. This can take time for the person that has been violated to clear off their credit report and to restore money back into their bank or credit card accounts.

Some ways you can prevent identity theft is to check your financial information on a regular basis. Check your bank account and credit card statements thoroughly for any discrepancies or charges you didn't' transact. In addition, keep copies of your banking and financial records. Ask for a copy of your credit card report to review if anyone opened or used any accounts in your name. Do not give your personal data out to just anyone. If someone calls asking for any personal data, have them send you something in writing to document who they are if they need that data.

If you find your identity has been stolen, you can request a credit freeze and cancel any debit or credit cards. This should be done right away. Get a copy of your credit report and create an identity theft report that will help you get the fraudulent activity removed from your credit report. This will also notify companies that the debt is a result of identity theft. Preventative measures can be taken by contacting the credit reporting agencies and having them place a free fraud alert on your credit file. This will make it hard for anyone to open more accounts in your name.

Carolyn Goodwin, CPA PLLC ©

Lesson 10

Financial Risk

"A prudent person foresees danger and takes precautions. The simpleton goes blindly on and suffers the consequences." Proverbs 27:12

Let's define the word **risk**. **Risk** is an event or activity that will expose one to danger, harm, or loss. Let's think of some things that may be a risk in our daily lives. It can be anything from riding a bike, skateboarding, or driving in a car. In each of these examples, there is a risk associated. Some people even say there is risk in everything we do. How can we lessen the risk in the situations above? We can wear a helmet when riding a bike and skateboard. This is a way we can manage the risk. This is called **risk management**. It is a way to determine the risk associated with what you are about to do so that you can plan or devise ways to minimize or manage loss.

In the case of the risk of driving a car, the same can be done by wearing a seat belt or looking out for others on the highway. If you own a car, you are purchasing something valuable. The **financial risk** of owning a car would be having car repairs, someone taking your car (theft), or getting into an accident. These are called **financial risks** because there would be some out-of-pocket costs that you would have to pay on your own. A way to guard against this financial risk is to purchase **insurance** on your vehicle. **Insurance** is a risk management tool. It protects people from possible financial loss. It is a written document (**policy**) that lists the **terms** (description of

Carolyn Goodwin, CPA PLLC ©

what's covered and the dollar amount what will be covered) and the **premium payments** (how much you will have to pay to have the insurance policy).

There are several types of insurance available. Below are a few. In the lesson extension, you are encouraged to research different types of insurance.

- Life insurance
- Health insurance
- Long-term disability insurance
- Auto insurance
- Home insurance

Now we will put your knowledge of insurance and how it works into action…your call to action.

Carolyn Goodwin, CPA PLLC ©

YOUR CALL TO ACTION

Answer the following questions:

- What are some purchases that have financial risk?
- What are the risks associated with these purchases?
- Why is it a good idea to have insurance for these purchases?

Carolyn Goodwin, CPA PLLC ©

LESSON EXTENSION

- With your parent or guardian permission and help find an insurance quote comparison tool online. Determine an item of value you will be purchasing such as a home or a car. Research online to find out more about the coverage you need to have for your vehicle. Choose 2-3 options and determine which will be the better deal. Be sure the insurance is appropriate for your vehicle and the coverage you need. Use the sheet attached for your research.

  Purchase: ______________ **Value of purchase:** ____________________

  What are some risks associated with this purchase? What could happen to this purchase? ____

  ____

  ____

  ____

  Choose the two insurance options. Which one will you buy? Why?

  ____

  ____

  ____

  ____

- Determine a different scenario in which you would need insurance. Consider life insurance, health insurance that is not property. Explain the financial risk you could encounter and how the insurance will reduce your financial risk.

Carolyn Goodwin, CPA PLLC ©

Answer Key

Lesson 2

Gross Pay		$ 1,500.00	
FICA - Medicare	$1,500 * .0145	21.75	1.45%
FICA - Social Security	$1,500 * .062	93.00	6.20%
Total FICA tax		114.75	7.65%
****Net Pay (Take home Check)**		$ 1,385.25	

** This does not take into account any other payroll deductions such as retirement; or state and federal taxes, etc.

Lesson 3

Apartment Rent - $1,000	Need
Groceries - $150	Need
Eating Out - $100	Need or Want
Renter's Insurance - $12	Need
Utilities (gas, electric, water) - $100	Need
Cable - $50	Want
Internet - $50	Need or Want Depends on if it is needed for school or work.

Carolyn Goodwin, CPA PLLC ©

Lesson 4

Apartment Rent - $1,000	Fixed
Groceries - $150	Variable
Eating Out - $100	Variable
Renter's Insurance - $12	Fixed
Utilities (gas, electric, water) - $100	Variable
Cable - $50	Fixed
Internet - $50	Fixed
Pet care (food, litter, etc.) - $40	Variable

Carolyn Goodwin, CPA PLLC ©

Lesson 5

Income $2,500	$2,500.00
Fixed Expenses:	
Giving/donations	$250.00
Save	$250.00
Car Insurance - $80	$80.00
Apartment Rent - $1,000	$1,000.00
Renter's Insurance - $12	$12.00
Utilities (gas, electric, water) - $100	$100.00
Cable - $50	$50.00
Internet - $50	$50.00
Car Payment $250	$250.00
Groceries	$300.00
Eating Out	$75.00
Clothing	$83.00
	$2,500.00
Surplus/Deficit	$0.00
**This income does not take into account taxes withheld. '	

Carolyn Goodwin, CPA PLLC ©

Lesson 5 Extension

Savings Account A		
Initial Deposit	$ 250.00	
Interest Earned Year 1	$ 7.50	3%
Account Balance	$ 257.50	
Interest Earned Year 2	$ 7.73	3%
Account Balance	$ 265.23	
Interest Earned Year 3	$ 7.96	3%
3 Year Account Balance	$ 273.18	
Savings Account B		
Initial Deposit	$ 300.00	
Interest Earned Year 1	$ 6.00	2%
Account Balance	$ 306.00	
Interest Earned Year 2	$ 6.12	2%
Account Balance	$ 312.12	
Interest Earned Year 3	$ 6.24	2%
Account Balance	$ 318.36	
Interest Earned Year 4	$ 6.37	2%
Account Balance	$ 324.73	
Interest Earned Year 5	$ 6.49	2%
5 Year Account Balance	$ 331.22	

Carolyn Goodwin, CPA PLLC ©

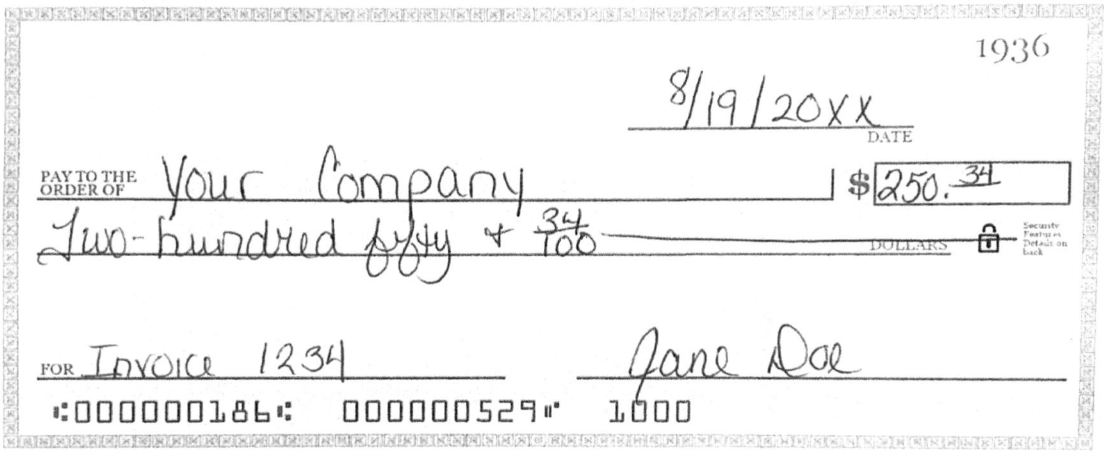
1936

8/19/20XX
DATE

PAY TO THE ORDER OF Your Company $ 250.34

Two-hundred fifty & 34/100 DOLLARS

Security Features Details on back

FOR Invoice 1234 Jane Doe

⑆000000186⑆ 000000529⑈ 1000

Carolyn Goodwin, CPA PLLC ©

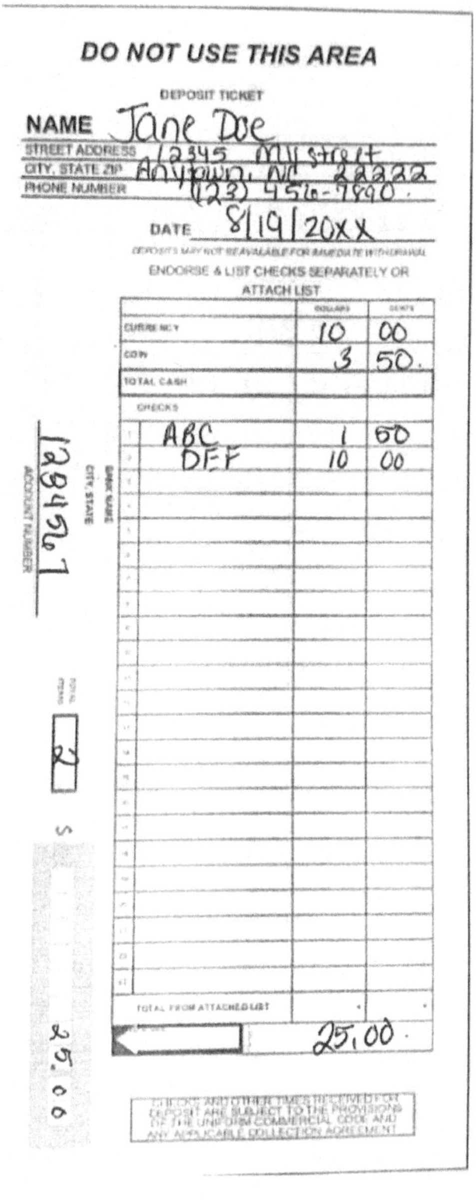

DO NOT USE THIS AREA

DEPOSIT TICKET

NAME Jane Doe

STREET ADDRESS 12345 My street

CITY, STATE ZIP Anytown, NC 22222

PHONE NUMBER (123) 456-7890

DATE 8/19/20xx

DEPOSITS MAY NOT BE AVAILABLE FOR IMMEDIATE WITHDRAWAL

ENDORSE & LIST CHECKS SEPARATELY OR ATTACH LIST

	DOLLARS	CENTS
CURRENCY	10	00
COIN	3	50
TOTAL CASH		
CHECKS		
1 ABC	1	50
2 DEF	10	00
TOTAL FROM ATTACHED LIST		
TOTAL	25.00	

BANK NAME

CITY, STATE

1234567

ACCOUNT NUMBER

TOTAL ITEMS 2

$ 25.00

CHECKS AND OTHER ITEMS RECEIVED FOR DEPOSIT ARE SUBJECT TO THE PROVISIONS OF THE UNIFORM COMMERCIAL CODE AND ANY APPLICABLE COLLECTION AGREEMENT

Lesson 6

Money market account	Lower Risk
Savings account	Lower Risk
Mutual fund	Higher Risk
Stocks	Higher Risk
Certificate of deposit	Lower Risk

- Bond gain = $550 ($500 + $50 interest) divided by $1000 cost = 55% rate of return. The bond was sold at a premium.
- Stock gain = $275 ($250 + $25 dividend) divided by $250 cost = 110% rate of return.

Carolyn Goodwin, CPA PLLC ©

Carolyn Goodwin, CPA PLLC ©

Made in United States
North Haven, CT
04 November 2026

21725770R00050